M000021766

The *Original Guide to Barbecue in the South* has been created in support of the Atlanta History Center's exhibition *BARBECUE NATION*, a chronicle of the cultural heritage and enduring influence of this great American foodway. Open to the public from May 2018 until June 2019, the exhibition includes a wide array of pitmaster artifacts, barbecue ephemera, oral histories, vintage photographs and a series of special events. For full exhibition information, visit *atlantahistorycenter.com*.

In partnership with YETI

ATLANTA
HISTORY
CENTER

Atlanta History Center
130 West Paces Ferry Road NW
Atlanta, GA 30305

BARBECUE NATION
May 2018—June 2019

CONTENTS

The Original Guide to Barbecue in the South

NO FLAME IN THE PIT

IN 1954, JOURNALIST RUFUS JARMAN was on assignment for *The Saturday Evening Post,* exploring the deep-rooted culture of barbecue in the South. "Every true barbecue chef agrees," Jarman wrote, "that no flame should be tolerated in the pit." While Jarman was being literal—defining the specifics of half-burned coals capped with whitening ash—his words point out perhaps the most important axiom of barbecue in America. That barbecue is more than meat and fire. It is more than a meal. It is an American art form. It is a passalong genius. Its masters mind the pit, stoke its coals, stay up all night, swabbing the splayed hogs and secreting away pinches of this and dabs of that. It is a language in smoke. And for as long as hungry folks have walked the American South, from the eastern edges of the Carolinas, to the tiny towns of Arkansas, up to the Shenandoahs in Virginia and down into Georgia pinewoods, barbecue has been our founding foodway. While preferences will evolve and techniques will vary, over decades and across county lines, what abides is a sense that barbecue, good barbecue at least, has the power to unite us all. -*Taylor Bruce*

ALMANAC

A Short History of Barbecue, Pitmasters of Note,
Neon Signs, Homemade Sauces, Barbecue and the Blues,
Zora Neale Hurston, Civil Rights and more.

A SHORT HISTORY OF BARBECUE

1707 .... *First account of New World barbecue appears in Ned Ward's* The Barbacue Feast

1766 .... *British-appointed Governor of NC throws barbecue in Wilmington, Sons of Liberty toss the meat into the river*

1793 .... *To celebrate new U.S. Capitol cornerstone, George Washington roasts an ox*

1870 .... *15th Amendment ratified, grants African-Americans the right to vote*

1891 .... *Golden Rule Bar-B-Q opens in Irondale, AL*

1895 .... *Harper's Weekly cover shows men turning hogs over coal pit at Cotton States Exposition*

1897 .... *Ellsworth Zwoyer patents the charcoal briquette*

1907 .... *Steamboat cook Henry Perry moves from Memphis to Kansas City*

1909 .... *Possum barbecue in GA honors newly elected William Howard Taft*

1916 .... *Sid Weaver sets up first barbecue tent in Lexington, NC*

1922 .... *Leonard Heuberger sells first pulled pork sandwich for five cents in Memphis*

1925 .... *Bob Gibson invents white sauce [mayo-vinegar-apple juice] to keep smoked chickens moist*

1948 .... *Heinz begins selling a bottled barbecue sauce*

1948 .... *Piedmont Airlines offers in-flight meal of Rogers Barbecue on Charlotte to London flights*

1964 .... *Ollie's Barbecue in Birmingham files lawsuit against Civil Rights Act, loses 9-0 in Supreme Court decision*

1978 .... *First World Championship Barbecue Cooking Contest held in Memphis*

1980 .... *Jimmy Carter serves Augusta's Sconyers Bar-B-Que at White House*

1981 .... *McDonald's debuts McRib sandwich to mixed reviews and parody*

1985 .... *Charlie Vergos advertises 1-800-Hogs-Fly hotline in* The Wall Street Journal, *delivers his Memphis ribs via FedEx*

1986 .... *Controversial "Truth in Barbecue" law passed by SC legislature*

1995 .... *JJ's Rib Shack name-checked by Atlanta rap group Goodie Mob*

1996 .... *Oscar Poole, of Ellijay, GA, carries Olympic torch in his Pig Moby-il*

1999 .... *Author John Egerton establishes Southern Foodways Alliance*

2004.... *McClard's in Hot Springs, AR alters recipes and portion sizes after Bill Clinton's heart bypass surgery*

2012 .... *Volunteers rebuild Sam's Bar-B-Q in Humboldt, TN after devastating fire*

2015 .... *Anthony Bourdain spotlights Rodney Scott's whole hog expertise on CNN*

POLITICS & BARBECUE

From county sheriffs to U.S. Senators, barbecue and politics have been longtime southern tablefellows. In the early decades of American democracy, hosting political barbecues grew from normal stump-speeching to moments of social revelry. In some instances, these potluck political gatherings wallowed into all-day, rowdy shindigs, where electorate and candidate both imbibed in gratuitous amounts. Whiskey and gristle led to winning votes. One Alabama anti-barbecue reformer, disgusted by his witness of the amalgam, wrote a series of columns in the 1820s for Huntsville's *Southern Advocate* newspaper. Using the penname Barbacuensis, the critic chided that the good citizenry should "turn at last from shote and grog" for fear of "suicidal indulgence." As the *Advocate* saw it, the gluttonous gatherings where elected officials swapped swigs of moonshine chasing their own ambitions pointed the democracy towards "fatal gales of the stormy seas of barbecue politics." It was a depraved scene, Barbacuensis warned, turning to poetry to describe the pitfalls of a typical affair.

> *Did'st ever see a Barbacue? For fear*
> *You should not, I'll describe it you exactly:*
> *A gander-pulling mob that's common here,*
> *of candidates and soveren stowed compactly,*
> *Of harlequins and clowns with feats gymnastical*
> *In hunting shirts and shirt-sleeves — things fantastical;*
> *With fiddling, feasting, dancing, drinking, masquing*
> *And other things which may be had for asking.*

For a deeper study of politics and barbecue, read
Mark A. Johnson's An Irresistible History of Alabama
Barbecue: From Wood Pit to White Sauce.

ICONS OF NOTE

*Visionaries who laid the foundation for
contemporary barbecue culture in the South*

JOHN "BIG DADDY" BISHOP AL

*Built original Dreamland [by
hand] in 1958, same year Paul
"Bear" Bryant came to Tuscaloosa*

....

LYTTLE BRIDGES NC

*After Red passed in 1966, "Mama
B" ran Red Bridges Barbecue
Lodge for 42 years strong*

....

ROBERT LEE "BIG BOB" GIBSON AL

*Former L&N railroad worker,
giant of 'cue [6'4", 300 pounds]
invented Alabama white sauce*

....

PETE JONES NC

*Opened Skylight Inn in 1947 when
he was 19, starting family line of
Ayden pitmasters*

....

WALTER JONES AR

*Circa 1910s, Jones Bar-B-Q Diner
is one of the region's oldest black-
owned restaurants*

....

JACK O'DELL SC

*Opening year of Midway BBQ isn't
quite clear, O'Dell's "Hash King"
moniker is undisputed*

....

**RAYMOND AND
DESIREE ROBINSON** TN

*In 1977, Cozy Corner founders
moved from Denver to set up this
tiny family-run shop in Memphis*

ADAM SCOTT NC

*Local minister sold out of his own
back door, launching the gospel of
Goldsboro BBQ*

....

WAYNE SHADDEN AR

*Until it closed in 2010, Shadden's
Grocery off Highway 49 was a
must-stop for BBQ pilgrims*

....

HOUSTON SPRAYBERRY GA

*Once pulled pork sandwiches out-
sold the diesel pumps, Sprayberry's
Bar-B-Q was born*

....

WARNER STAMEY NC

*Jess Swicegood pupil bought his
teacher's joint and tutored other
pitmasters for decades*

....

**SID WEAVER AND
JESS SWICEGOOD** NC

*Early practitioners of "Lexington-
style" pitched smoke tents across
from the courthouse*

....

BRADY VINCENT TN

*Origin point for "barbecue spa-
ghetti," a curiosity still on the menu
at Memphis' Bar-B-Q Shop*

....

CHARLIE VERGOS TN

*Memphis-style ribs began inside
the coal chute basement of Vergos'
downtown eatery*

[*Charlotte, NC*]

[*Gray, GA*]

[*Memphis, TN*]

[*Shelby, NC*]

[*Birmingham, AL*]

[*Richmond, VA*]

Across every decade of American music, barbecue has found the lyric sheets, from Louis Armstrong's "Struttin' With Some Barbecue" to Widespread Panic's "Ribs and Whiskey." And quite often, barbecue was a backdoor to more risqué topics, especially with blues singers in the 1930s and 40s. Blues legend Lucille Bogan, who recorded the song "Barbecue Bess" in Chicago in 1935, was a master at smoky insinuations. For proof, see the lyrics below.

> *When you come to my house, come down behind the jail*
> *I got a sign on my door, "Barbecue for Sale"*
> *I'm talking about my barbecue, only thing I crave*
> *And that good doing meat going to carry me to my grave*
> *I'm selling it cheap, because I got good stuff*
> *And if you try one time, you can't get enough*
> *I'm talking about barbecue, only thing I sell*
> *And if you want my meat, you can come to my house at twelve*

SAUCES ACROSS THE SOUTH

Carolina Treet • Wilber's Barbecue Sauce • Big M's Hot & Thick Sauce • Slap Sauce • Carolina Sunshine Tangy Barbecue Sauce • Pappy's Hottest Ride in Town • Mrs. Griffin's Barbecue Sauce • Sweet Georgia Soul • Holy Smoke BBQ Sauce • Georgia On My Mind Sauce • Blues Hog Barbecue Sauce • Wild Rooster Mustard Mania Sauce • Smokey C's White Sauce • Harold's Hog Wash • Punchin' Pig Sauce • Outta the Park BBQ Sauce • Bone Doctors' Original • Barbecue Sauce • Jack's Old South Hog Sauce • Shealy's Bar-B-Que Sauce • Scott's Barbecue Sauce • Bone Suckin' Sauce • Moonlite Original BBQ Sauce • Alabama Salvation Sauce • Lillie's of Charleston "Hab Mussy" Sauce • Bezzie's Home Style Hot-N-Spicy • Bootsie's • Hot as Funk BBQ Sauce • Don's Best Sauce • Ward's Kentucky Specialties • Kentucky Smokin' Sauce • Pappy's Moonshine Madness • The Smoke Doctor's Hot & Spicy Sauce • Popa Sisco's Arkansaw Hog Sauce • Coach Sposato's Bar-B-Que Sauce • Cannon's Pig Paint BBQ Sauce

ZORA NEALE HURSTON

Their Eyes Were Watching God

"Y'all know we can't invite people to our town just dry long so. I god, naw. We got tuh feed 'em something, and 'tain't nothin' people laks better'n barbecue. Ah'll give one whole hawg mah ownself. Seem lak all de rest uh y'all put tuhgether oughta be able tuh scrape up two mo'. Tel yo' womenfolks tu do 'round 'bout some pies and cakes and sweet p'tater pone."

The women got together the sweets and the men looked after the meats. The day before the lighting, they dug a big hole in back of the store and filled it full of oak wood and burned it down to a glowing bed of coals. It took them the whole night to barbecue the three hogs. Hambo and Pearson had full charge while the others helped out with turning the meat now and then while Hambo swabbed it all over with the sauce. In between times they told stories, laughed and told more stories and sung songs. They cut all sorts of capers and whiffed the meat as it slowly came to

perfection with the seasoning penetrating to the bone. The younger boys had to rig up the saw-horses with boards for the women to use as tables. Then it was after sun-up and everybody not needed went home to rest up for the feast.

By five o'clock the town was full of every kind of a vehicle and swarming with people. They wanted to see that lamp lit at dusk. Near the time, Joe assembled everybody in the street before the store and made a speech.

"Folkses, de sun is goin' down. De Sun-maker brings it up in de mornin', and de Sun-maker sends it tuh bed at night. Us poor weak humans can't do nothin' tuh hurry it up nor slow it down. All we can do, if we want any light after de settin' or befo' de risin', is tuh make some light ourselves. So dat's how come lamps was made. Dis evenin' we'se all assembled heah tuh light uh lamp. Dis occasion is something for us all tuh remember tuh our dyin' day. De first street lamp in uh colored town. Lift yo' eyes and gaze on it. And when Ah touch de match tuh dat lamp-wick let de light penetrate inside of yuh, and let it shine, let it shine, let it shine. Brother Davis, lead us in a word uh prayer. Ask uh blessin' on dis town in uh most particular manner."

While Davis chanted a traditional prayer-poem with his own variations, Joe mounted the box that had been placed for the purpose and opened the brazen door of the lamp. As the word Amen was said, he touched the lighted match to the wick, and Mrs. Bogle's alto burst out in:

We'll walk in de light,
de beautiful light

Come where the dew drops of
mercy shine bright

Shine all around us by
day and by night

Jesus, the light of the world.

They, all of them, all of the people took it up and sung it over and over until it was wrung dry, and no further innovations of tone and tempo were conceivable. Then they hushed and ate barbecue.

Renowned as a folklorist, anthropologist and fiction writer, Zora Neale Hurston focused her research and published work on the complexities of the African-American experience in the South, from politics and gender roles, to foodways and spirituality. Her 1937 novel, Their Eyes Were Watching God, *sells more than half a million copies annually to this day.*

THE CIVIL RIGHTS MOVEMENT

During the 1950s and 60s, barbecue restaurants in the South served as home-bases of resistance to racial segregation and Jim Crow, from feeding movement leaders to sparking landmark court cases. Below are a few notable examples.

ALECK'S BARBECUE HEAVEN
Atlanta, GA

Regarded as MLK's favorite spot [he was fond of the "Come Back Sauce" ribs], Aleck's was next door to West Hunter Street Baptist, home church of Ralph Abernathy.

BIG APPLE INN *Jackson, MS*

Medgar Evans, the heroic NAACP field secretary in Mississippi, rented an office above the shop, often meeting with advocates over pig ear sandwiches downstairs.

BRENDA'S BAR-B-Q PIT
Montgomery, AL

Opened in 1942, this carry-out joint was true to the idea of barbecue as "rebellion food," using their own copy machine to print flyers for NAACP meetings in the 1960s.

HOP'S BAR-B-QUE
Asheboro, NC

Lesser known than the lunch counter sit-ins 25 miles north in Greensboro, student protestors from Asheboro desegregated the 21-seat joint in January 1964.

LANNIE'S BAR-B-Q *Selma, AL*

Lannie Moore Travis fed civil rights workers and City Hall employees alike while delivering sandwiches to fuel the nearby Freedom House residents and Brown Chapel congregation.

MAURICE'S PIGGIE PARK
West Columbia, SC

The Supreme Court ruled in favor of a class-action lawsuit in 1964, but infamous owner Maurice Bessinger continued to champion Confederate beliefs until his death in 2014.

OLLIE'S BARBECUE
Birmingham, AL

Owners challenged the Civil Rights Act's constitutionality in attempt to deny service to black patrons, losing in unanimous 9-0 verdict at the U.S. Supreme Court.

PEACHES RESTAURANT
Jackson, MS

Willora "Peaches" Ephram ran her soul food haven for five decades on Farish Street, a hub for black leaders. Ms. Peaches was known to take meals to activists in detention camps.

"OLLIE MCCLUNG'S BIG DECISION"

LIFE MAGAZINE
October 9, 1964

Ollie McClung is a self-effacing 48-year-old lay preacher of the Cumberland Presbyterian Church in Birmingham, Ala. who runs a barbecue restaurant on State Highway 149 on the seedy south side of the city. At lunchtime the 220 seats in Ollie's Barbecue fill up quickly with a loyal clientele that includes corporation executives in dark suits and laborers in work clothes. At night men come and bring their families. Ollie's menu describes the barbecue as "the world's best," and the many customers who agree with this have made Ollie well and respectfully known in his neighborhood. Now Ollie has become well-known far from the south side—throughout the U.S. He is the first man to challenge the Public Accommodations section of the civil rights law and win. Hearing the case of Ollie McClung Sr. & Ollie McClung Jr. v. Robert Kennedy, a three-judge panel of the federal district court last month held the Civil Rights Act unconstitutional as applied to businesses not engaged in interstate commerce. They ruled that Ollie, whose customers are virtually all local, is not so engaged. [In another case, involving a motel catering to interstate businesses, courts have upheld the law.] If the Supreme Court upholds him and the lower court, Ollie McClung will have struck a historic blow for segregation.

In December 1964, the Ollie's case went before the Supreme Court. Justice Hugo Black, of Alabama, who was once a member of the Ku Klux Klan, voted against the segregationist challenge. His opinion clashed with that of his wife, Elizabeth; she was a regular at the restaurant. The original south side location of Ollie's closed in 1998.

BRUNSWICK STEW DEBATE

VIRGINIA House Joint Resolution No. 35   *January 19, 1988*

WHEREAS, the celestial sustenance known as Brunswick Stew first appeared on earth in Brunswick County, Virginia, in 1828; and

WHEREAS, this gustatory invention was fathered by camp cook Jimmy Matthew's divine inspiration and mothered by the necessity of feeding the hunting parties of Dr. Creed Haskins of Mount Donum on the banks of the Nottoway River; and

WHEREAS Brunswick Stew's bucolic ingredients originally included squirrel, bacon, onions, butter, salt, pepper, and stale bread, all boiled together; and

WHEREAS, when the hunters returned to this simple repast they expressed skepticism, but upon partaking of the pastoral creation they exclaimed with wonder and asked for more; and

WHEREAS, the legend of Brunswick Stew has spread across America, giving rise to specious and wicked accounts of its origin; and

WHEREAS these pernicious blasphemies must be stopped.

GEORGIA House Resolution No. 906   *February 25, 1988*

WHEREAS, for eighty-odd years, the Battle of the Brunswicks regarding the origin of the robust ragout known as Brunswick stew has stewed in every cauldron of controversy from gazette to government house; and

WHEREAS, the legendary fine tastes of our northerly neighbors have easily enticed them to ingest great quantities of this culinary concoction; and

WHEREAS, the epicurean egos of the Famed Feasters of Virginia have understandably lured them to covet the credit for Georgia's renowned reflection; and

WHEREAS, in spite of the audacity of competing claims, the City of Brunswick, Georgia, has excellent evidence for establishing its affirmation of authorship of this savory soup; and

NOW, THEREFORE, BE IT RESOLVED BY THE HOUSE OF REPRESENTATIVES that the members of this body do hereby officially recognize the City of Brunswick, Georgia, as the birthplace of Brunswick stew and affirm Brunswick, Georgia's claim to this culinary concoction.

INTERVIEWS

Helen Turner, Martell Scott II,
Nick Pihakis, Bryan Furman, Lucille Anderson,
Frank Horner and Sam Jones.

HELEN TURNER

PITMASTER

Helen's Bar-B-Que
Brownsville, TN

NOT MANY PEOPLE in Tennessee cook open-pit and don't use anything but wood.

IF IT'S DRY WOOD, that's some good cooking right there.

YOU DON'T GET ADJUSTED to the smoke. I tried goggles. I tried the little mask thing over your face. It all irritates me.

I'VE BEEN OPERATING by myself since 1996. I ain't gotta tell nobody "Get over there, get out of my way."

SUNDAY IS THE ONLY day I get off.

MY HUSBAND comes in around 5am to make the fire, and I get here about 7am and put the shoulders on.

EVERYBODY ASKS "Well, Helen, why don't you expand?"

WHY? Because some of my customers don't even want my daughter to fix their sandwich.

THEY SAY, "Where's Helen? She knows how to fix my sandwich. She knows how I like it."

A LOT OF PEOPLE love the flavor and don't want any sauce. Just meat and bread.

THIS BUILDING is about 120 years old.

WE'VE HAD THREE serious fires. I fought it until the fire department got here.

PASSING something on is important.

I GOT SEVEN grandchildren, and they claim, if it gets down to it, they would want to run this place. But you can't take over anything if you're not here to learn it.

THE SMOKE, the dust, all of that. It's hard work. I do it because I love it.

MARTELL SCOTT II

SAUCE MAKER

Scott's Barbecue Sauce
Goldsboro, NC

THE RECIPE came to my grandfather in a dream.

HE WAS A MINISTER, and sold barbecue out of his backyard. He did it the old-fashioned way, taking oak coals and cooking the pig over it.

MY FATHER had Scott's Barbecue Sauce patented in 1946.

HE BOTTLED it in the kitchen and sold to mom-and-pop stores here in Goldsboro.

I FIRST TASTED it when I was six.

IT'S THIN and vinegar-based. We never got into that thick, heavy or sweet stuff.

THE FIRST CHAIN that took it was the Winn Dixie in Raleigh in 1951.

I STILL REMEMBER when we got a machine that could bottle 12 at once, 48 in a minute.

AFTER FOUR YEARS active duty in the Air Force, I came home and took over the sauce business. That was June 1968.

IN THE BUSY SEASON, we sell 24,000 bottles a month.

EVEN NOW, we do most of it by hand. Not this high-tech stuff. We label it, cap it, date it, box it and put it in the warehouse.

ONLY THE FOUR SCOTT men have ever done the pepper mixing and sauce making.

IN 1961, someone broke into our old building. When police were searching the place with flashlights, they saw a head pop up from inside one of our wooden sauce barrels.

TURNED OUT it was half full.

DAD TOLD POLICE, "The man got that sauce on him and those peppers got in his skin. He's suffered enough."

NICK PIHAKIS

RESTAURATEUR
Jim 'N Nick's BBQ
Birmingham, AL

IN 1985, my father retired from the insurance business, and he said, "Nick, why are you working for somebody else. Let's open up our own restaurant."

....

WE FLIPPED A COIN and decided to do a barbecue restaurant.

....

OUR FRIEND Phillip Adrey taught us everything.

....

PHILLIP worked at Ollie's Barbecue. He was 72.

....

THE GREATEST leaders deeply believe in what they're doing. People will follow that.

....

HE SHOWED ME how it was done. About moving the meat around on the pit, about learning the fire.

....

EVERY NIGHT, around 8:30pm, Phillip would go out to his car and pour himself a bourbon, and he'd wipe his table down and tell me about his philosophy of cooking barbecue, why it was an art.

....

WE'VE GOT 40 restaurants now, doing 150 million dollars a year.

....

I STOPPED running from the fact that we're a big company. We can do things for the community that smaller companies can't do.

....

I GET TO HAVE intimate conversations with men and women, about taking over family restaurants, how hard that can be. Anything I can do to contribute, I want to.

....

YOU KNOW the saying "You've got big shoes to fill"?

....

WHEN YOUR grandfather starts something 70 years ago and people come in and they go "Oh, Mr. Jones isn't here anymore. Is the food going to be as good?"

....

I TELL THEM to stand up and be proud to say, "It's better."

BRYAN FURMAN

PITMASTER

B's Cracklin' Barbeque
Atlanta, GA

COOKING is a sense. Senses and feelings.

MY DAD always said, "If you can't control the fire, you can't cook meat."

I LEARNED whole hog cooking through trial and error.

WE GREW UP slaughtering pigs in South Carolina. And when I started researching heritage breeds in 2011, I didn't see any barbecue joints doing that.

I WAS A WELDER for 10 years before we opened B's Cracklin'.

I SAVED UP my 401K money, and we opened up the first shack for 15 grand.

GOOD BARBECUE joints run out of food. Shitty joints don't. That might not be good to put in a book, but that's what I say.

I'VE NEVER taken shortcuts.

I'M A DUDE from South Carolina making barbecue in Georgia. Our peach mustard sauce is that combination.

EVERY GUY I know that burns their coals down, they are at the restaurant 24/7.

FOR ALL OUR new guys, just watch me start the fire. I don't want you starting anything.

SOMETHING DIFFERENT every day. Last week my wood guy left the tarp off and it started to rain. So I jumped up from bed and ran to the restaurant before anyone.

MY FAVORITE JOINT is 30 minutes from my grandmother's house. It's called Campbell's Quick Stop in Rembert, South Carolina.

WHEN YOU GET an ego and think you're the best, then you get your ass knocked off the top.

LUCILLE ANDERSON

WAITRESS

Abe's Barbecue
Clarksdale, MS

I STARTED working at Abe's on March 23, 1998.

IF WE NEED to fill in, I'm going to fill in that spot. It's like one big family here.

THE FRONT ROOM is mostly booths. In the middle room, we have four booths and six tables. The back room is tables only.

THERE ARE FLYING PIGS on the ceiling, pictures of barbecued pigs, people that have been in before.

I TOOK A PICTURE with Morgan Freeman the first time he came in. He ordered a sweet tea and a pork plate.

A LOT of regulars come in two or three times a week.

TODD GETS a barbecue plate with double slaw. He always wants a chili cheeseburger, but he had heart surgery.

TODAY, he came in and told me, "The doctor said I could have a teaspoon of chili," so that's exactly what I gave him. A teaspoon of chili.

RUSTY FROM First National Bank always gets barbecue, fries and a Coke. His wife Anne, she gets the tamales and her lemonade.

I'LL ALWAYS tell you, "If there's something wrong, let me know." That's what I'm here for.

I DON'T WANT you to go out and say you're not coming back because something went wrong.

AT ABE'S, we're in the middle of the Delta, right at the Crossroads.

I DON'T KNOW anything about Robert Johnson. He sold his soul to the devil here, but that was before my time.

FRANK HORNER

BARBECUE JUDGE

Memphis in May
Memphis, TN

MEMPHIS IN MAY is the grand-daddy. It's the world championship. Has been for 40 years. The world championship of barbecue.

TO BE A JUDGE, Memphis in May has a class once a year.

IT'S ABOUT six hours. There are some tests involved.

TASTE is something that cannot be taught.

HOG, SHOULDER AND RIB are the three categories. It's all pork. That's all Memphis in May does.

ALL JUDGES score on the same criteria: appearance of the entry, tenderness of the entry, flavor and then an overall impression score.

FOR THE HOG, I personally am looking for a mahogany color. It's a little bit darker than gold en. Can you visualize that?

A SHOULDER ENTRY is a good place to look for a smoke ring.

YOU WANT to make sure the smoke penetrated the skin and got down into the meat.

IT GOES FROM very dark down to almost red.

FOR RIBS, you're looking to make sure that the meat hasn't pulled away from the bone and dried out. That it comes off the bone with a little bit of tug, but that you don't have to bite it with your teeth or take a knife to get it off.

EVERYTHING should be eaten with the finger.

YOU GET A REALLY, really good bite, and you just sit back and close your eyes and don't wanna leave.

I TELL YA, I've gotten spoiled over the years.

SAM JONES

PITMASTER

Skylight Inn and Sam Jones BBQ.
Ayden, NC

BARBECUE is geography. It's completely dependent on the piece of dirt where you're standing.

....

CHOPPED PORK, coleslaw and cornbread. At the Skylight Inn, ninety percent of guests are gonna get that.

....

PAPER BOAT or on a bun. Those are your options.

....

I WAS STANDING in the kitchen at Skylight Inn one Saturday a few years back. It was busy. And I saw this farming family, the McLawhorns, standing in line. Mr. J.B. McLawhorn, his two sons, Johnny and Shea, and his grandson Johnny Mac, who was holding his young son.

....

IT JUST HIT ME: That's four generations of family right there.

....

I ASKED, "Mr. J.B., how long you been eating here?" And he thought nothing about it. He said "Sam, I ate my first sandwich here in 1951."

MY FIRST JOB at the Skylight was wiping off tables and filling the drink box.

....

MY GRANDDADDY Pete didn't have a lot of education, and when I say "a lot" I'm talking about third grade. He could only write his name, and he couldn't read.

....

I WAS ALMOST 16 before I was aware of that.

....

SKYLIGHT SITS on the original Jones family farm. That's why: The land was free.

....

ONE OF MY great uncles landed a small plane on the airship next door, and when he came close to the building some of the roofing boards flew off. He walked over and asked my granddaddy, "You thinking of putting skylights in?"

....

WE GET THREE phone calls a week asking about our room rates.

NOTHING TOOK PLACE without my granddaddy's blessing.

WORKING WITH my granddaddy and my dad, sometimes it felt like a zoo full of elephants running around in the joint. Everybody pissed about something.

I REMEMBER the mailman in Ayden, standing at the counter one day at Skylight, telling my granddaddy how to make a million dollars. My granddad was standing there smoking a cigarette, and when that man walked out, he just looked at me and he said, "Son, if you wanna make a million dollars, talk to the man that made a million dollars. Don't talk to the mailman."

THE TURTLE didn't get on the fence post by himself.

WE TAKE a whole animal, between 175 and 190 pounds, and cook it over a bed of oak coals for about 18 hours.

IT'S CHOPPED and then it's lightly seasoned. Salt, pepper, a dash of hot sauce and apple cider vinegar.

THERE'S ONLY ONE other place I'd recommend to get an accurate depiction of eastern North Carolina barbecue. And that's Grady's in Dudley, North Carolina.

MR. GRADY'S in his eighties now, and there's no real succession plan. There's no next generation. When he draws his last breath, and they write his obituary, they'll have to write two.

MY GRANDDADDY used to say: "If something happened to me this place would close up in six months."

WHEN HE DIED, it was in all the papers and on the news. "Barbecue Legend Dies at 77." And we lost 25% of our business.

HE DIDN'T CREATE a perception in the community that he'd trained us all well.

THEN THE Southern Foodways Alliance did a film on the Skylight, and they screened it at the Big Apple BBQ Fest in New York City.

ALL THE GUESTS stood to their feet and applauded.

WE'D BEEN COOKING hogs a long time in Ayden, North Carolina to no applause.

I REMEMBER walking around thinking, "How in the world did you get here?"

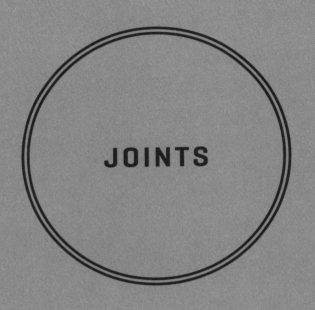

JOINTS

The 40 establishments listed here — old guard and new school, small town and big city — tell the pit-smoked and sacred story of barbecue in the South.

NOTE: *Texas is not included in our coverage of the South. For Louisiana and Florida, we did not select any establishments as emblematic of the regional canon.*

ALABAMA

BIG BOB GIBSON BAR-B-Q AL

Alabama white sauce. There's maybe nothing more iconically Alabama—or more confounding to out-of-staters—than this mayo based, pepper flecked concoction. And Big Bob's is ground zero. For more than 90 years, ever since the lumbering Bob Gibson first hand-dug a pit and tacked oak planks to a sycamore tree in his backyard for a makeshift table, that tangy white sauce has gilded pit-smoked chickens in this little town on the banks of the Tennessee River. Today, it makes cameos in joints from the Shoals to Mobile Bay, but the OG version at Big Bob's remains boss.

Chris Lilly, the current pitmaster, who married into this house of 'cue—and has tucked more than a few BBQ World Championships under his belt—serves the whole gauntlet [pulled pork, ribs, smoked turkey and even brisket]. But the chickens, split, spiced and laid bare on the long brick pits for three and a half hours before they get dipped whole into a vat of white sauce, are especially worth crowing about.

FIND: 1715 6th Ave SE [Hwy 31], Decatur
CALL: 256 350 6969

SAW'S BBQ AL

At the barbecue altar, Saw's offers non-denominational respite: barky pulled pork, smoky chicken quarters, and pit-perfect ribs coexist on plastic-foam trays. At the other Saw's outposts, Soul Kitchen and Juke Joint, the sweet-tea brined fried chicken, boudin and charred wings are worthy of a tent revival. Before Saw's, Mike Wilson worked in Cooking Light magazine's test kitchens. On weekends, he stoked his barbecue dreams. So much so, when word got out of a local joint closing shop, he snatched up the lease and opened two weeks later. Saw's has been smokin' ever since.

FIND: 1008 Oxmoor Rd, Homewood
CALL: 205 879 1937

DREAMLAND BAR-B-QUE

Tuscaloosa is all about pageantry. And this African-American-owned rib shack, opened in 1958, the same year Paul "Bear" Bryant joined the Crimson Tide, proves that ribs, sauce, and a couple of slices of white bread are all you need to build a legacy.

FIND: *5535 15th Ave, Tuscaloosa*
CALL: 205 758 8135

MISS MYRA'S PIT BAR-B-Q

Hickory smoke from the indoor brick pit gives patina to this Cahaba Heights joint and a mottled mahogany crust to its barbecue chicken [served with white sauce, of course]. Don't skip the cooked custard banana pudding.

FIND: *3278 Cahaba Heights Rd, Birmingham*
CALL: 205 967 6004

BOB SYKES BAR-B-Q

Van Sykes, son of Bob and brick pit torchbearer, firmly believes Alabama barbecue is hickory, pork and tomato-based sauce. His smoldered and glazed spare ribs will quiet anyone who disagrees.

FIND: *1724 9th Ave N, Bessemer*
CALL: 205 426 1400

TOP HAT BARBECUE

When Wilbur Pettit, a former bread delivery man, bought Top Hat in 1967 he had to pay extra for the sauce recipe. Good thing he did. It's that sauce and green hickory smoke that give his pork shoulders their swagger. No seasoning. No rub. Just a 3:30 a.m. start time and a cord of wood.

FIND: *8725 US Hwy 31, Blount Springs*
CALL: 256 352 9919

[*Dreamland Bar-B-Que*]

ARKANSAS

McCLARD'S BAR-B-Q

You can eat in if you want to. You can stride across the checkerboard floor and plop yourself down in one of the red swiveling stools that line up like soldiers along the Waffle House-style countertop. And you can order the ribs to stay. The dry ribs, maybe. Or the wet ribs, red with sauce. Ribs with slaw and beans. Ribs under a blanket of fries. You might even order a side dish of tamales, because they do that here, and you can eat it all on site. McClard's has been serving Central Arkansas since 1928, and you might well want to pay your respects in person.

Or here's an idea: Order takeout from McClard's and bring it with you to Hot Springs National Park, which is but a short half-mile away, and spread it all out for a picnic. Or take it down the road just a bit to Lake Hamilton, and eat it while you fish. Or go a touch further west to the Ouachita National Forest, and stash it at your campsite in a bear-proof cooler. With McClard's serving 7,000 pounds of meat a week, you need never be out in the wilderness on an empty stomach.

FIND: *505 Albert Pike Rd, Hot Springs*   CALL: 501 623 9665

CRAIG'S BAR-B-Q

Lawrence Craig's joint is so historic that, in 1997, it was honored at the Smithsonian Festival of American Folklife. Today his son, Robert, serves super-sauced ribs along with sandwiches so sloppy they come wrapped in wax paper.

FIND: *15 W Walnut, DeValls Bluff*   CALL: 870 887 2616

JONES BAR-B-Q DINER

Reputed to be the South's oldest black-owned restaurant, it's the only Arkansas eatery ever to win a James Beard award. The family patriarch swore revenge from beyond the grave if his sauce recipe were to be revealed.

FIND: *219 W Louisiana St, Mariana*   CALL: 870 295 3807

GEORGIA

HEIRLOOM MARKET BBQ GA

It's tucked in a kind of suburban hollow, half-hidden by a thundering interstate, scrappy pines and a dazed-seeming magnolia. It's attached to a convenience store that advertises beer and lottery tickets. Amid Atlanta's sprawl, this passes for secluded. The provenance of Heirloom Market BBQ is as unlikely as its location. The husband-and-wife operation pairs a hillbilly chef born in Texas, raised in Tennessee and trained in Atlanta with a former Korean pop star turned roots-food adventurer.

The result: a West-meets-East comingling that reflects an evolving America. Like jazz or hip-hop, barbecue is an indigenous art open to reinterpretation. While that's long meant mustard sauce versus vinegar-based sauce in the Carolinas, or beef in Texas and pork everywhere else, Heirloom takes an existential leap. Gape at the offerings: kordova sandwiches piled with gochujang-marinated pork and topped with ssam sauce and kimchi kale; 12-hour, miso-injected brisket; tempura sweet potatoes. There are OG beats, too: North Carolina pulled pork; Brunswick stew; sweet tea [ok, jasmine sweet tea]. Patrons dine standing at tall patio tables while smoke pours from a stove pipe as if from a back-woods still. Finished, full, feeling damn lucky, head next door for a lottery ticket.

FIND: 2243 *Akers Mill Rd, Atlanta*
CALL: 770 850 1008

B'S CRACKLIN' BARBEQUE GA

Ever bitten into a cloud of sauce-drenched wood smoke? That's the bliss of eating Brenda's Brisket Sandwich, or any locally sourced plate at B's Cracklin' Barbeque. With an everybody-knows-your-name atmosphere, Atlanta and Savannah locations are relative newcomers tending pure traditions.

FIND: 12409 *White Bluff Rd, Savannah*
CALL: 912 330 6921

FRESH AIR BARBECUE GA

Somewhere between here and there, Fresh Air is roadside country barbecue at its throw-back-iest. The no-frills menu muses on pulled pork and Brunswick stew. Period. An ancient brick pit rises inside like a head at Stonehenge—the real, mystic deal.

The joint's origins echo a common storyline for barbecue longtimers. Its first incarnation was opened in 1929 by a local veterinarian who sold barbecued rabbits on weekends. In 1945, after the original owner died, manager George "Toots" Caston bought the place and went whole hog, literally, cooking them 19 deep on the pits. For travelers taking the two-lane highway from Atlanta to Macon, the smoky smell was too good to pass up. Luckily in the 70 years since not much has changed.

FIND: 1164 Highway 42 South, Jackson
CALL: 912 330 6921

SOUTHERN SOUL BARBECUE GA

Flip-flops-meet-craft-beer BBQ. Diners eat among sea breezes, palmetto trees and piled-high cords of hickory. 'Cue cooked inside this converted gas station is aimed at genre-bending connoisseurs: PBR beer cheese soup, anyone? Smoked oyster spread? Barbecuban? Worth the 12-mile pilgrimage off I-95.

FIND: 2020 Demere Rd, St. Simons Island
CALL: 912 638 SOUL

HOLCOMB'S BAR-B-Q GA

Want to go local? Head to Holcomb's outside-of-town locale. Looks like a wood shed from the outside, a revival camp canteen behind the screen door: two long tables, sawdust floors. Only open Fridays and Saturdays.

FIND: 7070 Highway 15 South, White Plains
CALL: 706 467 2409

[*Fresh Air Barbecue*]

KENTUCKY

MOONLITE BAR-B-QUE INN

Mutton and burgoo—served in fewer than 10% of Kentucky's barbecue places, predominantly in a few counties in western Kentucky—top the list of Kentucky's distinctive regional cue, and Moonlite stands as a longstanding shrine to both. Mutton, the smoked meat of mature sheep, cooks on huge custom pits fired by hickory wood for 15 to 18 hours. Pit tenders keep mutton quarters moist and seasoned by basting hourly with a "black dip" of water, Worcestershire sauce, vinegar, lemon juice, black pepper, brown sugar, allspice and garlic. Chopped mutton is amply fatty and makes a mean sandwich. You can order mutton sandwiches and plates [the latter comes with cornbread muffins, pickles and onions], but the groaning board buffet allows a sampling of hickory-smoked mutton and burgoo—a tangy, slow-simmered slurry of mutton, chicken, cabbage, potatoes, corn and tomato puree—which pairs well with the smoky meats. Owner Patrick Bosley, whose grandfather bought Moonlite in 1963 when it was a small diner, calls the buffet "an extension of grandmaw's table."

FIND: 2840 *W Parrish Ave, Owensboro*   CALL: 270 684 8143

KNOTH'S BAR-B-QUE

This homey roadside diner serves outstanding pulled pork—the primary west Kentucky barbecue—from shoulders that cook 24 hours on well-seasoned pits fired by hickory coals. Come for the smoky succulent pork and bask in 1965-era charm. Open March through November.

FIND: 728 *US 62, Grand Rivers*   CALL: 270 362 8580

R&S BAR-B-Q

Thinly sliced pork steaks grilled over hickory coals and sopped with vinegar-lard-pepper "dip" distinguish the unusual barbecue found in Monroe and a few nearby counties. Get a shoulder plate "sprinkled" or "dipped" for extra spice. Eat with your fingers and sop the dip with pork pieces and white bread.

FIND: 217 *S Jackson St, Tomkinsville*
CALL: 270 487 1008

MISSISSIPPI

UBON'S

A lot of barbecue restaurants will tell you that if the meat's good enough, you don't need sauce. Ubon's might argue that if the sauce is good enough, you barely need meat. Ubon's sauce uses a family recipe dating back five generations, to the days when it was made in a wash tub and stirred with a boat paddle, and it derives from one Ubon Roark, whose irrepressible granddaughter—Leslie "The Barbecue Princess" Roark—helps run the business today. It's "half tomato and half vinegar," she says, with none of the artificial flavoring known as liquid smoke. "We feel like if you're gonna have something taste smoky, then for the love of God burn something." Ubon's sells its sauce around the country alongside its Bloody Mary mix, which originated as a hybrid of the barbecue sauce and dry rub. The Ubon's team would have one of those libations going while working the pit at barbecue competitions, and eventually it became popular enough to bottle and sell in its own right. As for the meat, Ubon's mostly sells brisket, smoked for four hours and wrapped to contain the juices—then cooked another five hours, at least, to tenderize.

FIND: 7501 *MS-57, Ocean Springs*   CALL: 228 875 9590

THE SHED BARBECUE & BLUES JOINT

Rebuilt after a 2012 fire, the family-run Shed occupies a sprawling 10,000 square feet near the Gulf. Most of the meat smokes over pecan. The house specialties are live music and rib racks.

FIND: 7501 *MS-57, Ocean Springs*   CALL: 228 875 9590

LEATHA'S BAR-B-QUE INN

Leatha Jackson sold her first slab of beef ribs in Foxworth, gaining smoke-cred throughout the Pine Belt in the 1970s. Fast forward 30 years, she opened shop on Highway 98 outside Hattiesburg. Her upright smoker is tended today by grandson Brian Jackson, who slathers the famously mysterious marinade over all.

FIND: 6374 *US 98, Hattiesburg*   CALL: 601 271 6003

NORTH CAROLINA

BUXTON HALL

Tradition is a wonderful thing, but sometimes it can just feel so...traditional. Located in the progressive, creative mountain town of Asheville, Buxton Hall opened in 2015 with the notion to modernize the restaurant experience without losing the old-school cooking techniques that make barbecue taste like barbecue.

Pig-wise, Buxton is all about whole hogs cooked over wood. Same as it ever was in North Carolina. But beverages move way beyond sweet tea: There's a proper cocktail program, including house slushies of bourbon mixed with Cheerwine. The restaurant also has its own pastry chef, the esteemed Ashley Capps, whose banana pudding comes in the form of a pie [complete with a vanilla-wafer crust and a torch-toasted meringue]. Food arrives on ceramic plates, as opposed to stuffed into Styrofoam clamshells.

Buxton Hall is housed in the old Standard Paper Sales Company building, which had stints as a roller-skating rink and a boat showroom before becoming a cue joint. The space is a physical reminder that nothing stays the same forever. And sometimes, if you're lucky, what comes next might improve upon what came before.

FIND: *32 Banks Ave, Asheville*
CALL: 828 232 7216

SKYLIGHT INN

Many folks think this whole-hog joint, dating back to '47, makes the absolute best chopped-pork sandwich in America. The capitol of barbecue, they call it. You'll know you're there when you see a brick building with a model of the U.S. Capitol on the roof.

FIND: *4618 S Lee St, Ayden*
CALL: 252 746 4113

[*Grady's Barbecue*]

LEXINGTON BARBECUE NC

The cathedral of "Western style" barbecue serves pork shoulders every day but Sunday. If you're just passing through, they'll bring you curb service. Impress a local by calling the joint by its nickname, Honey Monk.

FIND: 100 *Smokehouse Ln, Lexington*
CALL: 336 249 9814

WILBER'S BARBECUE NC

Shaped like a roadside motel, Wilber's is to Eastern N.C. as Lexington is to Western: pretty dang close to definitive. The headline item is the Pit-Cooked Barbecue Pork Plate with coleslaw, potato salad and hush puppies.

FIND: 4172 *US-70, Goldsboro*
CALL: 919 778 5218

GRADY'S BARBECUE NC

An African-American institution since July 4, 1986, Grady's serves pork plates out of a modest white cinderblock building with a Pepsi sign out front. It's a true mom-and-pop shop, run by Steve and Gerri Grady. Say hi; they'll be there.

FIND: 3096 *Arrington Bridge, Rd, Dudley*
CALL: 919 735 7243

JACK COBB & SON BARBECUE PLACE NC

Cobb started off as a door-to-door barbecue seller, and even now the restaurant is open peculiar hours [Wednesdays, Fridays and Saturdays] and sells only takeout. If you want the pork, you play by their rules. Get an extra pound to freeze.

FIND: 3883 *S Main St, Farmville*
CALL: 252 753 5128

SOUTH CAROLINA

SCOTT'S BAR-B-QUE SC

No one means more to South Carolina barbecue than Rodney Scott, the pitmaster and restaurateur so devoted to his craft that he doesn't just cook whole hogs all night over wood—he cuts the wood himself with a chainsaw. Scott operates from an old slant-roofed country store [color scheme: white and robin's egg blue] that has over time become a pilgrimage site. [Anthony Bourdain and Andrew Zimmern, among others, have made the trip.] He opens at 9:30 a.m. Wednesday through Saturday and asks that no one try to get their pork any earlier than that. In 2017, he opened his second restaurant, Rodney Scott's BBQ, on King Street in Charleston. This new place does fancy things like accept credit cards. But the principles [whole hogs, cooked slow over wood] remain the same. Even though South Carolina is known for mustard sauce, Scott uses a pepper-vinegar-citrus recipe handed down from his father, Roosevelt "Rosie" Scott, believing that mustard is better used for hot dogs. Longtime customers know to request their pork sandwiches with a slab of crackling skin, which has the texture of a potato chip. Scott himself likes to stuff his meat into a slice of white bread and eat it like a taco.

FIND: 2734 Hemingway Hwy, Hemingway
CALL: 843 558 0134

JACKIE HITE'S BAR-B-Q SC

A championship South Carolina high-school football player in 1958, Jackie Hite was a whole-hog legend until his death in 2016—so much so that he won three terms as mayor. Hite was also the Leesville fire chief for ten years. It was through Fire and Rescue barbecue fundraisers that Jackie discovered his love for real wood 'cue. His namesake restaurant soldiers on serving mustard-sauced pork in the mornings and early afternoons.

FIND: 460 E Railroad Ave, Leesville
CALL: 803 532 3354

SWEATMAN'S BARBECUE

It's not every day that you find an all-you-can-eat barbecue joint: In the case of Sweatman's, it's just Fridays and Saturdays. They're closed the rest of the week, giving customers time to digest their whole-hog 'cue basted in mustard sauce. Bub Sweatman opened his barbecue homestead in 1977, way out in the country. If it weren't for the white, pig-shaped sign by the highway, passersby would think the place was just an old wood-plank farmhouse. Soon after Sweatman built the pits, Holly Hill resident Douglas Oliver caught on as a meat cutter, training under a pitmaster named Chalmon Smalls. Oliver shoveled coals and tended the slow-roasting hogs from dusk to dawn—for nearly four decades—becoming a master at his craft, though less heralded. In October of 2017, Douglas Oliver passed away, a true legend of Carolina barbecue.

FIND: 1427 *Eutaw Rd, Holly Hill*
CALL: 803 496 1227

HOME TEAM BBQ

The downtown location is open until 1 am, and the later it gets the likelier you are to order fried ribs with Alabama white sauce and "death relish." Arrive earlier for the ribs, pulled pork and homemade sausage. And in a town full of fancy restaurants, even highfalutin chefs can't deny the addictive deliciousness of Home Team's chicken cracklins. Not exactly barbecue, but who's judging.

FIND: 126 *William St, Charleston*
CALL: 843 225 7427

BROWN'S BARBECUE

The secret sauce at Brown's is something called "barbecue gravy," a pepper-vinegar blend that goes on the hogs during the cooking process—and may also wind up on your collard greens. Brown's serves buffet-style, so be patient in that line. Their busy day is Sunday.

FIND: 809 *Williamsburg County Hwy, Kingstree*
CALL: 843 382 2753

[*Sweatman's Barbecue*]

TENNESSEE

CENTRAL BBQ

It takes an awful lot to make an impression on the Memphis barbecue scene—this city needs another rib shack about as much as it
needs another Elvis impersonator. And yet, in 2002, Craig Blondis
and Roger Sapp decided to give it a go. They'd been veterans of the
competition circuit [which culminates in the summertime pork fest
known as Memphis in May], so they knew their way around a pit. And
after they opened their first restaurant in Midtown, you could smell
the smoke from down the block. Given all the touristy cue around
town, they billed themselves as the locals' choice. Two more locations followed, with plans to franchise across the South. And the key
at all of them is cooking slow. Very, very slow. The wings take three
days. The ribs—the famous ribs, the ones that ship around the country for $45 per rack—are marinated for 24-hours, dry-spiced and
slow-smoked over hickory and pecan. By the time they hit the plate,
they're mahogany. Pulling them apart offers no resistance. They have
been cooked into submission.

FIND: 2249 *Central Ave, Memphis*
CALL: 901 272 9377

HELEN'S BAR-B-Q

The irrepressible Helen Turner runs her joint more or less by her-
self, piling pork sandwiches high onto a white bun, dousing them
with a mahogany sauce and stabbing them shut with a toothpick. Also
available: Barbecued bologna. One of only a few female pitmasters in
America, Helen Turner keeps things simple at her clapboard, roadside joint. Since she bought the place in 1996, she has started most
mornings by checking the fire and laying pork shoulders on the open
brick pit. Every day but Sabbath Sunday smoke billows out of the
screened-in back porch. Amen.

FIND: 1016 *N Washington Ave, Brownsville*
CALL: 731 779 3255

[*Charlie Vergos' Rendezvous*]

MARTIN'S BAR-B-QUE JOINT

The kings of Nashville-area barbecue cook a whole hog every day. Their joint has no freezer. No microwave either. Everything's made from scratch, right down to the chips.

FIND: 7238 *Nolensville Rd, Nolensville*
CALL: 615 776 1856

PAYNE'S BAR-B-Q TN

Running the restaurant as a tribute to her late husband Horton, owner Flora Payne serves overstuffed chopped-pork sandwiches dripping with daffodil-yellow slaw. This being Memphis, she does ribs too.

FIND: 1762 *Lamar Ave, Memphis*
CALL: 901 272 1523

CHARLIE VERGOS' RENDEZVOUS TN

If you're staying at the Peabody Hotel, cross the street and head down the alley until you see the striped awning. Descend into the basement. You've just found America's most famous dry-rubbed ribs—a tradition since 1948. Trust the fine gentlemen in black bowties working the floor—Demetrius, Hollyrock, Pooh, Geno, Big Jack, Robert Junior [his dad worked here for 53 years]. They are all barbecue legends in their own right.

FIND: 52 *S. 2nd St, Memphis*
CALL: 901 523 2746

SCOTT'S-PARKER BBQ TN

Old-timers may know this low-slung roadside haunt as B.E. Scott, but the restaurant has been in the Parker family for two generations now. Expect whole hogs cooked 24 hours. If you like the sauce, you can get it to go in a mason jar.

FIND: 10880 *US-412, Lexington*
CALL: 731 968 0420

VIRGINIA

Q BARBECUE

Few barbecue restaurants have celebrity chefs. Usually, the star is the pig. But in the Richmond area, a man named Tuffy Stone has become a kind of barbecue prophet after an extraordinary run on the competition circuit. Stone [along with his team, Cool Smoke] has won more than 40 grand championships. He's conquered Memphis In May. The Jack Daniel's World Championship Invitational. The Kingsford Invitational. A track record like that gives a man a certain reputation. Tuffy has by opening five Q Barbecue restaurants in the Richmond area. They serve pork, chicken, brisket, ribs—the works. He also offers one unusual side: something called "pineapple hot dish," a kind of baked, buttery upside-down cake. Should you eat there and decide you want to replicate his cue at home, Tuffy has also opened an institute of higher learning called BBQ School, a series of weekend-long seminars where aspiring pitmasters can learn about equipment, presentation, and smoke management, plus "rubs, injections, sauces, brines & spritzes." Plan ahead: The classes sell out months in advance, even at $750 a head.

FIND: 2077 *Walmart Way, Midlothian*   CALL: 804 897 9007

KING'S BARBECUE

Down near the Appomattox River, the third generation of Kings are cooking meat in the Virginia style. In business since 1946, they're known for pork shoulder smoked 12 to 14 hours over white oak and served with an uncommon vinegar-tomato-mustard sauce.

FIND: 460 *E Railroad Ave, Leesville*   CALL: 803 532 3354

FRITH'S DIXIE PIG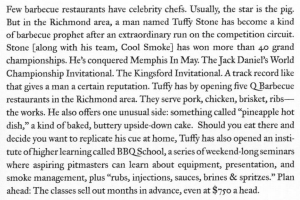

You have two choices at Frith's: the chopped pork tray or the sliced pork tray. Both come with fries and hush puppies and allow Instagram privileges in front of the classic neon sign with the grinning porker.

FIND: 817 *Memorial Blvd N, Martinsville*   CALL: 276 632 9082

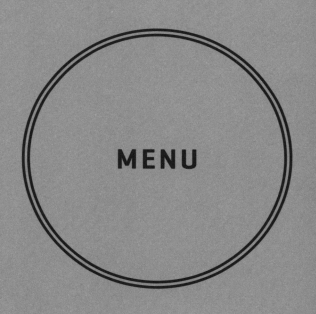

MENU

While barbecue norms can change from town to town, these five offerings stand out in what they add to the canon of Southern 'cue.

PULLED PORK SANDWICHES

Pork on a bun remains the definitive barbecue dish—
a foodway at the heart of North Carolina

WHILE EVERYONE in North Carolina agrees that pork is the only meat that matters, the western part of the state serves shoulder sandwiches and the eastern part goes whole hog.

You're guaranteed to get a pepper-vinegar sauce in North Carolina. Out west, toward the Piedmont, that sauce will be blushing pink with ketchup.

Eastern NC barbecue is pulverized almost to mush, and sopping wet with its sauce. But the Western NC version has more structure.

BOTH SANDWICHES come with finely chopped slaw, making these the rare barbecue sandwiches that finish with a crunch.

TRY A PLATE

Skylight Inn — Ayden, North Carolina
Grady's — Dudley, North Carolina
Wilber's — Goldsboro, North Carolina

RIBS

*Primal eating at its finest, a rack of ribs demands
a massive appetite and a stack of wet-naps*

THOUGH BEEF RIBS are delicious and Flintstonian, the default
position in the South is that plain-old "ribs" refer to pork.

*A properly cooked rib will
be splotched with black char.
Without it, the rib may
appear pale and wan.*

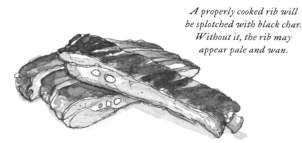

MEMPHIS IS TO RIBS as
Detroit is to automo-
biles: Good ones are
made elsewhere, but
civic pride runs particu-
larly deep there.

*To tenderize their ribs, many
pitmasters will marinate before
cooking—fruit juice is not
unheard of—and then baste
with sauce, using a kitchen mop,
during the hours over a flame.*

TRY A PLATE

Big Bob Gibson BBQ — Decatur, Alabama
12 Bones Smokehouse — Asheville, North Carolina
The Rendezvous — Memphis, Tennessee

BRUNSWICK STEW

*Usually served as a side, stew can
easily scale up to an entree*

THE ONLY SOUP of note in the barbecue universe, Brunswick stew either has origins in Brunswick, Georgia or Brunswick County, Virginia, depending on who you ask.

Traditional stews will feature chicken and usually pork—both shredded—alongside corn, potatoes, and butter beans in a sweet tomato sauce.

As with barbecue itself, a proper stew can cook all day over a low heat to develop its flavor.

A PROPER STEW should be thick enough to eat with a fork. A shake of hot sauce never hurt it.

TRY A BOWL

Fresh Air Barbecue — Jackson, Georgia
Alberta General Store & Deli — Alberta, Virginia
Sand Fly — Savannah, Georgia

WHITE BREAD

*Even if you order a BBQ platter, as opposed to a sandwich,
you'll still likely get bread on the side*

....

*White bread functions
as equal parts:*

CONVEYANCE DEVICE
EDIBLE NAPKIN
SAUCE MOPPER

....

*White bread becomes
more common the
closer you get to
Texas, where it comes
standard virtually
everywhere.*

AS IT MINGLES with your barbecue juices, your bread will begin
to disintegrate. This is your cue to eat more quickly.

Never attempt to substitute wheat, rye, pumpernickel or any
bread made with a whole grain. Wonder Bread is as fancy as
you want to get.

TRY A SLICE

Dreamland — Tuscaloosa, Alabama
The Shed — Ocean Springs, Mississippi
Cozy Corner — Memphis, Tennessee

BANANA PUDDING

The only reason not to gorge yourself on barbecue is because you're saving room for this stuff

THE BARBECUE WORLD'S signature sweet—often the only dessert on offer—is built around coin-shaped banana slices nestled into a thick custard.

FANCIER PUDDINGS *are topped with meringue. Homestyle ones get whipped cream. Still others arrive naked.*

For texture, you'll usually find either ladyfingers, sponge cake, or [most commonly] vanilla wafers.

Always ask your server if the pudding is made in house. If it's not, just order extra pork instead.

TRY A BOWL

Fox Bros. Bar-B-Q — Atlanta, Georgia
Hill's Lexington Barbecue — Winston-Salem, North Carolina
Buxton Hall — Asheville, North Carolina

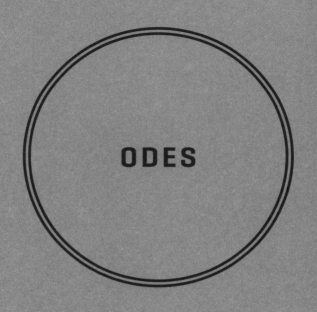

ODES

---

*Four writers of note bring the story of barbecue to life
through short essays and an original poem.*

THE JOINT

by Drew Jubera

They're found in cow pastures and alleys, in strip malls and off lonely ribbons of two-lane, across the street from churches and auto repair shops and jails.

———

The barbecue restaurant—or joint or place or shrine—remains something at once scattered and ubiquitous, as vivid in our collective imagination as it is on the American landscape. To find one, chase your nose. The scent of smoking wood—oak, hickory, mesquite—is as reliable as any GPS. It'll pull you up Jug Factory Rd., in Tuscaloosa, to Dreamland, or deep in the heart of Texas, to City Market, in little Luling. The sign out front will be hand-painted and unfussy, or neon and aflame. Older establishments tend to be low-slung aggregations of roadhouses, bingo parlors and gas stations. [Sweet Daddy's, in Mississippi, offers fill-ups along with rib tips.] Inside blooms a BBQ biosphere—a 'cue-centric world where dark is light, smoke is air, meat is God. Some interiors are pioneer-plain, like indoor camp grounds: a counter, sawdust floor, tables, chairs. Red-checkered tablecloths pass for pizazz. The setting is as Paleolithic as the meal, and just as transporting. Others display rec-room baroque—wood-paneled walls smeared with the whimsy of pilgrims and locals alike: license plates and pennants and framed photos of youth league champs or epic drunk-fests. Neon signs glow like votive candles, as warm and welcoming as the embers out back. Barbecue's sacred rituals can commence.

You're home.

THE BLACK PITMASTER

by Lolis Eric Elie

It's hard to imagine it in this era of Barack and Beyoncé, Oprah and LeBron, but a generation or two before my own, black celebrities were so rare that news of a "colored" person on TV reverberated around the community.

In a nation that made it a priority to convince black people of our inferiority in myriad ways both large and small, all evidence of our equality was celebrated and welcomed. Evidence of black "superiority" was greeted as comfort sent by God.

In those days, black pitmasters fit into a certain category of superior beings.

The rise of celebrity pitmasters, all of whom are great cooks and most of whom are white, gives lie to the notion that any one race or ethnicity holds a monopoly on the skill of artfully smoking meat. Yet for generations barbecue was all but synonymous with black folks. Barbecue was hard, hot, dirty work and in the South, such tasks were relegated to black people by the whites who could afford to hire out. Black people could claim a certain amount of credit even for the quality of food at segregated white restaurants because black folks were often doing the cooking.

"There were [white] places that sold barbecue," Raymond Robinson, the late great pitmaster of Cozy Corner in Memphis said in my 2001 documentary, *Smokestack Lightning: A Day in the Life of Barbecue.* "They wouldn't serve us mostly, so that there's nothing you can say about that. But most of them had black cooks, so I imagine the food was good."

As a fan of good barbecue, I've rejoiced seeing fine-dining chefs and intrepid amateurs opening quality barbecue joints in places where previously none existed, whether in the South or further afield. Still, it pains me to realize that the rise of barbecue's national popularity coincides with a decline in the number of black pitmasters. There are good reasons for this. Black people born in the 1970s and 1980s have followed career paths that were all but closed to them before. It's natural that many would gravitate away from the fields to which their parents and grandparents were relegated. But there are bad reasons as well. The challenges of succeeding in the restaurant business are even more challenging for black pitmasters who are more likely to have difficulty attracting capital from [mostly white] banks and reviews from [mostly white] tastemakers.

So much of what it means to be black in America—the power and the pain and the celebration of it—resides within the layers of the pitmaster's art. I fear for the loss of that legacy. The cornerstones of American vernacular culture were laid by men and women, most of whose names we will never know. I want to remember whichever names we can, but several centuries of history have taught me to be suspicious. If the tradition of black excellence at the pit is not maintained and cultivated, historians of this great art will likely forget the African-American contribution to it. Kentucky was a slave state, which means black women did most of the chicken frying, yet a gray haired, white-faced man named Col. Sanders has been accepted as the face of this great Southern delicacy. I shudder to imagine that the face of Southern barbecue in the 22nd century will be similarly singular and light in complexion.

THE FULL PLATE

by Jennifer V. Cole

These are the sides. The accoutrements. The dishes that make barbecue into a meal.

————

Butter beans, simmered with lard until the thin casings barely contain their creamy filling. Macaroni noodles goaded with butter and cheese—cheddar, parmesan, Velveeta—into a gooey mass that gurgles in the pan and drips from the fork. Deviled eggs. Baked beans with meat. Or without. Potato salad, a hulking, lustrous mound that's flecked with pickle relish and chopped egg, awash in a low tide of mayonnaise and mustard.

Each side serves its purpose.

Green beans that luxuriate over the fire, catching fatty drippings from a whole hog at Buxton Hall in Asheville, at least give the illusion of healthfulness. [They're vegetables, aren't they?] Texture comes in the form of cracklins [which lend crunch to the pulled pork sandwich at Rodney Scott's in Charleston]. Vinegar-marinated slaw gives a hit of palate-cleaning acid. Braised greens studded with pork [but not too much pork] are the closest barbecue should ever come to salad.

The list goes on. Cheese grits. Lowcountry purloo. In Georgia or Virginia, a bowl of Brunswick stew. French fries. Hush puppies. Meat alone is not a meal, but we are not fussy when it comes to the food that rides shotgun. Hell, even a slice of white bread will do.

THE ALTAR

by Cathy Smith Bowers

When my guy sets before me
on our battered picnic table
a sinfully heaping plate of barbecue,

his once smooth choir-boy hands
charred from a long day's worship
at the altar of his grill, it doesn't matter

that all the saints his devout mother
named him for—Christopher, George,
and Patrick—have all since been

disrobed. Who cares about miracles
that can't be lifted to this ravenous tongue
by fingers drenched in the tangy ooze

of yellow or red, whichever he
has chosen for this age-old offering
of shoulder and shank. I share with him,

between bites of creamy coleslaw
and icy sweet sips of tea, something I
recently read about how this all got

started—a tree struck by lightening, its
single surviving ember drawing together
the tribe in a sacrificial feast of fear

and gratitude. But he is quick to disabuse
me, as he piles high again my plate,
delivering, between slurps of a cold one

he has just retrieved from the cooler, his
own more logical explanation. How
Prometheus, himself, was the one who

set it all in motion, braving the flaming
firmament to bring fire down to earth
so he could light the bright new grill

his woman had given him for Christmas.
But by now I'm laughing so hard I can't
muster the energy to argue his theory

of this ritual older than time. That brings
husband together with wife. Neighbor
with hungry neighbor. Whole clans on

pilgrimage to the nearest fair or festival
in search of this holiest of grails. Chopped
or sliced or pulled. On a bun so warm

and sloppy two fists cannot contain it.
My laughter is pierced by the sudden yelp
of our collie. I look up from my now empty

plate to see her catch upon her tongue
the hushpuppy my beloved has just tossed,
watch her circle once and then lie

down in the imaginary garden
of her own primal kind.

———

DREW JUBERA *is a five time Pulitzer-nominated journalist and has been a staff writer for Texas Monthly, The Washingtonian, and The Atlanta Journal-Constitution, where he was the national correspondent for nearly a decade. His pieces have appeared in The New York Times, ESPN The Magazine, and Esquire. He lives in Atlanta, Georgia.*

LOLIS ERIC ELIE *is a New Orleans-born writer and filmmaker. A former columnist for The Times-Picayune, he is the author of Smokestack Lightning: Adventures in the Heart of Barbecue Country. His writing has appeared in Oxford American, Gourmet, Bon Appetit, and The New York Times. He lives in Los Angeles.*

JENNIFER V. COLE *is a Mississippi-born writer and editor. Her work appears in Garden & Gun, Esquire, Travel + Leisure, and Fast Company. She was Deputy Editor of Southern Living, reporting on the South for nearly a decade. Most recently, she has been circumnavigating the globe, nonstop since spring 2017.*

CATHY SMITH BOWERS *is a native of South Carolina. She's published five collections of poetry including A Book of Minutes [2004] and Like Shining from Shook Foil [2010]. Her poems have appeared in The Atlantic Monthly, The Kenyon Review and Poetry. From 2010 to 2012, she was poet laureate of North Carolina.*

Wildsam is a travel brand and publishing house based in Austin, Texas. Our aim is to use the true stories of a place as the driver of more thoughtful discovery. We launched our signature series of travel guides in 2012. Blending evocative storytelling and bonafide expertise, the guides have garnered praise from The New York Times, Travel & Leisure, GQ, *and in 2015 won the prestigious Traveler 50 Award presented by* National Geographic.

Wildsam guides are sold nationwide in more than 400 independent shops and boutiques.

To learn more,
visit wildsam.com and follow @wildsam.

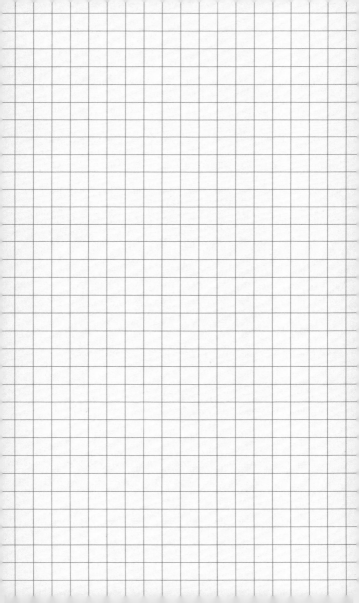